# Morning Routine
## *for*
# Night Owls

*How To Supercharge Your Day
With A Gentle Yet Powerful
Morning Routine!*

# Morning Routine
## *for*
# Night Owls

*How To Supercharge Your Day
With A Gentle Yet Powerful
Morning Routine!*

## S. F. Howe

Diamond Star Press
Los Angeles

**Morning Routine for Night Owls**: *How To Supercharge Your Day With A Gentle Yet Powerful Morning Routine!*

Copyright © 2018 by S. F. Howe
Published by Diamond Star Press

First Paperback Edition
ISBN 13: 9780977433513
ISBN 10: 097743351X

# Books by S. F. Howe

## Matrix Man
How To Become Enlightened, Happy And Free In An Illusion World

## The Top Ten Myths Of Enlightenment
Exposing The Truth About Spiritual Enlightenment That Will Set You Free!

## The Bringer Discourses
On Waking Up To The Mind Control Programs Of The Matrix Reality

## Secrets Of The Plant Whisperer
How To Care For, Connect, And Communicate With Your House Plants

## Your Plant Speaks!
How To Use Your Houseplant As A Therapist
*Coming Soon!*

## Vision Board Success
How To Get Everything You Want With Vision Boards!

## Sex Yoga
The 7 Easy Steps To A Mind-Blowing Kundalini Awakening!

**Transgender America**
Spirit, Identity, And The Emergence Of The Third Gender

**Morning Routine For Night Owls**
How To Supercharge Your Day With A Gentle Yet Powerful Morning Routine!

**When Nothing Else Works**
How To Cure Your Chronic Lower Back Pain Fast!

# Free Gift

As my thanks to you for reading *Morning Routine for Night Owls: How To Supercharge Your Day With A Gentle Yet Powerful Morning Routine!* I would like to give you the important bonus ebook, "Troubleshooting Resistance: How to Deal with the Stress of Change and Stay on Course to Achieve Your Goals."

Offered exclusively to readers of *Morning Routine for Night Owls,* this free report will enable you to overcome the resistance and procrastination that tends to arise sooner or later when you attempt to make lasting changes in your life. It is essential reading because it will give you the tools to stick with and reap the benefits of your new morning routine.

To download your free gift, just visit https://bit.ly/troubleshootingresistance/

For those who, in seeking solace from a noisy, crowded world, stay up late to enjoy the peace, silence and ineffable mystery of night.

# Table of Contents

# Introduction

## My Personal Story

I had a dream. It involved getting up early and carrying out a world class morning routine that would not only be good for me but would also make me feel good about myself and charged up about my day. I was convinced that if I could only start my day in this way, I would be amazing and have a perfect life. But there was a big problem. I was a night owl who went to bed late and woke up so groggy every morning, it took two hours or more to feel alert.

While high functioning morning larks jumped out of bed ahead of their alarms, meditated in the yoga headstand pose, and then, without needing a single sip of coffee, ran five miles, caught up on the news, made calls around the world, and crossed off half of their to-do list long before the work day had even begun in their time zone, my greatest morning exertion was hitting the snooze button over and over again, dragging myself out of bed and stumbling around drinking coffee with the nagging feeling that I was behind and had to 'catch up.'

Despite my passionate desire to conquer the mornings, the years passed and I never put my perfect morning routine into practice. In fact, things got worse before they got better. I reached a point where, for a time, I totally inverted my wake-sleep schedule while working from home. I slept during the day and stayed up until dawn. Of course, I levied any number of excuses at this behavior and really believed them.

On the positive side, I did all my creative and business-related work from the afternoon through the wee hours, did lots of meditation and evening exercise, and managed to lead a healthy and well-balanced life. But my relationships, both business and personal, subtly suffered because I would do anything to avoid a daytime appointment. When a daytime meeting couldn't be avoided, I would go into the morning or lunch meeting in a mild delirium, having never gone to sleep, then summon up all my resources to get through it, all the while feeling aghast at the brightness of the light and the perkiness of my fellowmen.

These patterns ended up limiting my business networking and my social life, although I convinced myself everything was okay. By placing myself out of alignment with the flow of daytime activity, I held myself back. Still I dreamed of the perfect morning – getting up early, performing a series of life-enhancing activities that would energize me and get me excited about my day, and then heading off into my day to be amazing.

Then one night I realized that I could still live my dream morning routine without becoming a morning person. That may seem obvious now, but at the time it was a novel thought! Right then and there I decided that I would put that perfect morning routine of my dreams into practice and carry it out every day after I woke up, no matter what the time.

As it turned out, that was a breakthrough moment. By experiencing a perfect start to my day, even though I was not getting up at the time I thought was the 'right time,' I felt better about my life and far more enthusiastic and energized about my goals. I was living my dream and receiving all of its benefits without having to change my circadian rhythms and become a morning person. Why hadn't I thought of this sooner?

One of the strange side effects of living my dream morning every single day is that without trying I started to get up a little earlier, and then even earlier still, until finally I realized that I was on the verge of becoming a morning person without ever intending to! No, I'm not there yet, but I have learned to love the early light of day and to long for more of it, which encourages me to get up earlier to enjoy it.

Perhaps you too are judging yourself harshly at some level for not being a morning person. Perhaps you too have held yourself back from starting your day in the ideal way for you because you thought you had to first change your wake-up time to an ideal early schedule. I am here to encourage you to start exactly where you are. Do not change a thing, except to add the joy of a morning routine to your day no matter when your day begins. Just read on, and I'll show you exactly how!

*Chapter 1*

# The Problem With Being A Night Owl

Everybody knows that it's better to be a morning person than a night owl, right? All our lives we've heard 'The early bird catches the worm,' or 'Early to bed, early to rise makes a man healthy, wealthy and wise.' The thing is, you know that this isn't you and is unlikely to ever be you.

While you're still rubbing the sleep from your eyes, nursing that first cup of coffee and grumping around the house, you're vaguely aware with a sense of mounting panic that morning people everywhere are popping out of bed like popcorn, pop, pop, pop.... you get the picture, then eagerly immersing themselves in a rapid series of mentally, physically and spiritually challenging tasks which culminate in their grabbing their sports bags and scurrying off for an intense workout at the gym.

All this before you have finished your first cuppa. To make matters worse, your eyes haven't even focused yet and maybe you've read the third paragraph in that top news article six times. Meanwhile the morning person has not only handily completed a holistic morning ritual that charged up every part of their multidimensional being, but has also arrived early at their workplace, bright eyed and bushy-tailed, ready to take on the world.

How can you, a night owl, win against this blatant demonstration of early bird power? You can't, so your best bet is to head back to bed for only 15 more minutes, at least that's what you promise yourself as you set the snooze alarm.

Jolting awake to a blaring newscast, you manage to drag yourself up and start the day your way – after all you only have 30 minutes to eat, shower, dress and go!

Probably you bought all the shiny books that promise to give you that unmistakable edge, if only you follow their system; just a simple ten part process that requires energetic goal-setting, athletic mind power techniques and a 'high intensity' workout, among other things. Or maybe they promise a short routine that requires you to leap from one step to the other like a frog on meth.

Okay, Night Owl, you may have bought the books, but most likely, they're just sitting on the shelf or on your hard drive gathering dust. But don't feel bad; the truth is, many a bona fide morning person, though tempted by all the promises in the books, end up ignoring them too. Why? Because most success books demand will power, which is hard for anyone to sustain, even morning people, and they motivate through fear by painting pictures of what you could lose to your more enterprising competitors, rather than focusing on helping you find your own rhythm and become more authentically you.

It's downright frustrating to hear all this pep talk about early bird success when you're a night owl who can barely manage to drag themself out of bed in the morning. If you're a true night owl, it's painful to even have to say hello to loved ones as you lumber around with squinty eyes and a scowling face, no matter how well you may love them at other times of day. If you're a dyed-in-the-wool morning grump, you probably negotiated with them for distance in the morn-ing, or, perhaps, they have learned through hard experience to avoid you like the plague.

A night owl is not only defined by how late they like to stay up and how much they like to sleep in; they are also identified by their general level of misery in the morning. If a good morning means you don't have to speak to anyone for at least the first two hours of the day, you are definitely a night owl no matter what schedule you're on.

Unfortunately, most of us night owls must, nonetheless, rise early to get to work, whether or not we tried to go to sleep at a reasonable hour or gave in and burnt the candle till the wee hours. Time doesn't stand still for anyone, least of all night owls. So for many, our nine to five work lives are a sham as we learn to masquerade as an early bird in a bright, glassy world, floating high energy and good cheer, while inwardly craving the calm, cool darkness of the forest.

Not only is it hard for night people to conform to the conventional workday orientation of our culture, the early scheduling often carries over to the weekend. Countless stoic owls can be found in every city in America suffering through their kid's 8 a.m. Saturday soccer practice or their Sunday morning church service. But how long can a person live in conflict with their natural biorhythm without it taking its toll?

To add insult to injury, most people judge night owls harshly and view them as suspicious, sociopathic, rebellious and/or dysfunctional. For many, it brings up images of crazed rock stars staying up all night partying and doing drugs, or serial killers using the cover of night to perform nefarious deeds.

The media further perpetuates the myth that lovers of the night are somewhat – okay, a lot – unsavory with its tales of vampires hunting the gloamy streets, loners hitting the bottle in the dark hours, or slackers playing brainless video games all night in their parents' basement.

Those of us who love the night know we would be harshly judged if ever it came out, therefore most sentence themselves to the closet, taking our night where and when we can, hiding the truth even from ourselves. Is there anything more terrible than a night owl in the closet?

But wait, there is good news. Psychological studies comparing morning people to night people reveal that owls are more creative, more intelligent, more original and more independent than early birds, which are all characteristics we should be proud of. Not only that, there is recent data that indicates night people are actually more financially successful than morning people. In chapter three, we will explore this and many more scientific discoveries about the differences between owls and larks, and you might be surprised by what you learn!

The purpose of this book is to help night owls living in an early bird world achieve the success they well deserve. Studies show that a good morning routine sets the tone for a successful and fulfilling day. The problem is that many night owls can barely get through their existing morning schedule, much less add additional tasks that could improve their life. This gives the early bird a distinct advantage because they naturally have high energy in the morning to invest in a powerful morning routine.

But don't despair, Night Owls. We've got your back! To help compensate for your lower morning energy, we have designed a gentle yet powerful morning routine that can be easily integrated into the first part of your day and that is guaranteed to supercharge your life. The following chapter explains why a morning routine matters so much, how it will help you, and why you should commit to doing it daily.

*Chapter 2*

# The Science Behind The Morning Routine

Morning routines have always been a part of our lives because everyone practices some kind of start of day ritual. On a typical weekday, you most likely get out of bed, take a shower, get dressed, eat breakfast, grab your keys and head out the door. Without doing at least that much, you would never get from your bed to your school or workplace, much less be presentable and ready to roll. And yes, those actions can definitely be considered your morning routine. However, the true power of a morning ritual to supercharge your life lies in the specific type of routine you practice.

Studies have shown that those who add certain positive habits to their morning schedule tend to be more successful, happier and healthier than those who don't. Once established, these habits contribute to increased energy, enhanced school or work performance and better relationships, resulting in a more successful and enjoyable life.

So what exactly are these positive habits? Though they may vary in the particulars, they are designed to work together to improve your mood and energy level, and create a positive attitude. The spiritually uplifting portion may include affirmations or prayer, reading inspirational books, visualizing, expressing gratitude and journaling. The focusing segment usually contains some form of goal-setting and meditation. The energy enhancing part of a routine typically involves the following: light housekeeping, exercising, personal hygiene, getting dressed and eating a healthy breakfast.

In this chapter, we will take a look at what science has to say about early day positivity and the various parts of a well-designed morning routine.

## Positive Attitude and Success

Studies reveal that creating positivity in the morning can be crucial to success throughout the day because it supports self-regulation. Self-regulation refers to the ability to manage your emotions, thoughts and behavior so that you act in your own best interests. Under the stresses and strains of everyday life, this ability tends to erode in the course of a day. In one 2007 study, researchers exposed some participants to a funny video or a gift and others to sad or neutral stimuli, and then tested their ability at self-regulation. The participants who experienced the happy events demonstrated better self-regulation as the day progressed. This indicates that if you make the effort to uplift your mood every morning, you are less likely to give in to disruptive emotions and impulses for the rest of the day, and more likely to act in a way that supports your core values and long-term well-being.

The question of whether happiness leads to success was tested in 2016 in a study by Drs. Lyubormisky and Diener that evaluated the effects of frequent positive affect on success. The researchers concluded that people who experienced more frequent and stronger feelings of happiness tend to have better health and more successful careers, marriages and friendships.

From these and the many other research findings on the importance of cultivating a positive attitude, you can feel confident in knowing that you will enjoy a more successful and happier life by taking time to develop the morning habits that uplift your mood. We have identified the best morning habits for the perfect start of day routine, and will share them with you in later chapters.

## Gratitude

Numerous studies reveal that writing down what you are grateful for increases well-being. Professors Robert Emmons from the University of California, Davis and Michael E. McCullough from the University of Miami investigated this phenomenon in 2003. In a study that included over 190 college students, researchers divided the students into three groups and made them fill out weekly reports on one of three topics: things for which they were grateful, things that hassled or irritated them, or general circumstances. These reports also included questions measuring the students' well-being. The evidence strongly indicated that the students expressing gratitude experienced a higher level of well-being.

According to Professor Craig Jackson, Chairman of Psychology at Birmingham City University, writing down what you are grateful for in the morning will help you notice and appreciate things that are more likely to make you happy, thus improving your mood and attitude towards life. A study by the University of California San Diego's School of Medicine further shows that people who express gratitude regularly have better health as measured by lower blood pressure, better immunity, better sleep, and better heart rhythm.

The research data on expressing gratitude supports the practice of writing down what you're grateful for during your morning routine, which we will discuss further in Chapter 6.

**Inspirational Reading**

In a study published in 2004, researchers from three American universities tested the effectiveness of reading as a mood booster; they compared reading a self-help book with individual therapy. From a sample of 31 adults at two senior living facilities in Alabama, some participants received 16 sessions of therapy while others read a book called *Feeling Good*. The results indicated that the readers had nearly identical results to those who attended the therapy, showing that your morning reading could help boost your mood as much as seeing a therapist! This data powerfully supports the practice of adding a few minutes of inspirational reading to your morning routine, which will be addressed in more detail in Chapter 6.

## Goal-Setting

Writing down your goals first thing may contribute to success according to a 2014 study by Dr. Gail Matthews of the Dominican University of California. Dr. Matthews wanted to find out what actions actually help people achieve goals. She recruited 149 participants for her experiment and divided them into five groups. Each group took progressively more action related to planning their goals. For example, the first group only thought about their goals, while the fifth group formulated written action plans and shared weekly progress reports with friends. All the groups that wrote down their goals saw greater success in achieving them, while the group that merely thought about their goals was the least successful in achieving goals.

This research supports the teachings of Edwin Locke, an American psychologist and pioneer in goal-setting theory. According to a study in 1981 by Locke and his team of psychologists, writing down your goals, no matter whether they are long-term or short-term, keeps you motivated, encourages you to take the next step, helps track progress, and helps you resist procrastination.

These are very important findings, and strongly support writing down your goals during your morning routine. We discuss this in detail in Chapter 7 on goal-setting, where we share our recommended technique.

## Organizing

In 2014, Navy Admiral William McRaven delivered an inspiring commencement speech at the University of Texas in Austin where he explained how making your bed could help you change the world. According to the admiral, making your bed in the morning is an easy task that may seem unimportant, but it sets a positive tone for the rest of the day, inspiring you to accomplish more complicated tasks.

Research supports how the simple addition of making your bed or unloading the dishwasher can actually improve your quality of life. A group of urban archaeologists at UCLA, interested in the average American home and its contents, published a fascinating book about the subject in 2017. Their long-term study of 32 families in California indicated that the presence of clutter and general disorder in the home literally increased the level of cortisol in mothers. Cortisol is also known as the stress hormone; a rise in cortisol can have serious effects on physical health over time, and has been correlated with hypertension, hyperglycemia and suppressed immunity. The clutter was also often a reason why families enjoyed their time together less.

The research suggests that not only does clutter contribute to your mental stress, but it can also affect your physical health. In Chapter 5, we discuss how adding a quick household reset to your morning routine offers a simple solution for this problem.

## Meditation

Meditation at the start of the day is important for managing your emotions and building coping skills. This helps you focus on current reality rather than worries or distractions. One 1998 study by researchers at the University of Arizona, required a group of stressed individuals (medical students) to engage in 8 weeks of meditation. The students experienced concrete benefits from the meditation including less anxiety, less depression, more empathy, and more spirituality. Significantly, the researchers were able to duplicate these results in another group of students, even observing additional benefits like increased mindfulness and improved coping by the participants during stressful examinations.

A morning meditation session increases your attention, focus, and ability to work under pressure according to a 2007 study conducted by three professors from the University of Pennsylvania's Department of Psychology. Another study by Eileen Luders and her colleagues at the UCLA Laboratory of Neuro Imaging confirms that meditation improves decision-making and information processing.

Meditation has important health benefits as well which have been noted by many researchers. In one recent review of three primary medical research databases by a team of physicians from Cyberjaya University College of Medical Sciences in Selangor, Malaysia, meditation is associated with a significant reduction in hypertension.

Meditation has also been found to help substance abusers control their addictions. In 2010, a group of Spanish researchers studied 34 individuals who had substance abuse problems. One group of 18 participants experienced seven weeks of goal management training combined with meditation. Another group of 16 only experienced standard treatment during the same time period. The individuals who participated in the meditation showed a stronger ability to control their addictive behavior.

In Chapter 8, we will be talking more about the importance of meditation during your morning routine, including how to meditate and the several types of meditation to choose from.

**Morning Exercise**

Many studies support the health value of exercising in the morning. According to a report by researchers at the University of Georgia, engaging in as little as 20 minutes of morning exercise for at least three days per week can help you feel more energized and less fatigued throughout the day.

Exercise increases libido, sexual energy and testosterone levels in men based on a study by Drs. Wiley, Bortz and Wallace at the Stanford University School of Medicine. Another study by psychologists Penedo and Dahn at the University of Miami links morning exercise to an increase in metabolism and fat loss.

Morning exercise, with the associated release of positive endorphins is crucial not only for physical health but also for mental health. Drs. Craft and Pena compiled results of medical studies spanning the nineties through 2003. After analyzing the data, they concluded that the type of exercise was far less important than the fact of exercise. In other words, any form of exercise improved the patient's mental well-being, giving them a greater ability to focus and a boosted mood. That is why, Night Owls, the gentle exercise we recommend for your early day routine in Chapter 9, will be just as effective as a more intense workout.

If you've always wondered why you're so different from the morning people in your life and wish you could be more like them, read on to discover the special abilities and qualities of night owls, as well as their unique challenges.

## Resources:

Alfonso, J., Caracual, A., Delgado-Pastor, L., & Verdejo-Garcia, A. (2011). Combined goal management training and mindfulness meditation improve execution functions and decision-making performance in abstinent polysubstance abusers. *Drug and Alcohol Dependence*, 117(2011).

Arnold, J., Graesch, A., Ragazzini, E., & Ochs, E. (2017). Life at Home in the Twenty-first Century: 32 Families open their Doors. Los Angeles, CA: The Cotsen Institute of Archaeology Press.

Bortz 2nd, W. M., & Wallace, D. H. (1999). Physical fitness, aging, and sexuality. *Western Journal of Medicine, 170*(3), 167.

Craft, L., & Perna, F. (2004). The Benefits of Exercise for the Clinically Depressed. *Primary Care Companion to the Journal of Clinical Psychiatry 6(3).*

Emmons, R., & McCullough, M. (2003). Counting blessings versus burdens: An experimental investigation of gratitude and subjective well-being in daily life. *Journal of Personality and Social Psychology, 84(2)*.

Floyd, M., Scogin, F., & McKendree-Smith, N. (2004). *Cognitive Therapy for Depression: A Comparison of Individual Psychotherapy and Bibliotherapy for Depressed Older Adults*. Behavior Modification 28(2).

Ivtzan, I., & Lomas, T. (2016). *Mindfulness in positive psychology: The science of meditation and well-being*.

Locke, E. A., Shaw, K. N., Saari, L. M., & Latham, G. P. (1981). Goal-setting and task performance: 1969–1980. *Psychological Bulletin, 90*(1), 125-152.

Luders, E., Kurth, F., Mayer, E. A., Toga, A. W., Narr, K. L., & Gaser, C. (2012). The unique brain anatomy of meditation practitioners: alterations in cortical gyrification. *Frontiers in human neuroscience, 6*, 34.

Lyubomirsky, S., King, L., & Diener, E. (2005). The Benefits of Frequent Positive Affect: Does

Happiness Lead to Success? *Psychological Bulletin, 131*(6), 803-855.

Mills, P. J., Redwine, L., Wilson, K., Pung, M. A., Chinh, K., Greenberg, B. H., & Chopra, D. (2015). The role of gratitude in spiritual well-being in asymptomatic heart failure patients. *Spirituality in clinical practice, 2*(1), 5.

Penedo, F. J., & Dahn, J. R. (2005). Exercise and well-being: a review of mental and physical health benefits associated with physical activity. *Current opinion in psychiatry, 18*(2), 189-193.

Puetz, T. W., Flowers, S. S., & O'Connor, P. J. (2008). A randomized controlled trial of the effect of aerobic exercise training on feelings of energy and fatigue in sedentary young adults with persistent fatigue. *Psychotherapy and psychosomatics, 77*(3), 167-174.

Shapiro, S., Schwartz, G., & Bonner, G. (1998). Effects of Mindfulness-Based Stress Reduction on Medical and Premedical Students. *Journal of Behavioral Medicine, 21(6).*

Study Focuses on Strategies for Achieving Goals, Resolutions. Retrieved from: https://www.dominican.edu/dominicannews/study-highlights-strategies-for-achieving-goals.

Swafford, T. Rhetorical Analysis of Retired United States Navy Admiral William Harry McRaven's 2014 Commencement Speech for the University of Texas in Austin.

Tice, D., Baumeister, R., Shmueli, D., & Muraven, M. (2007). Restoring the self: Positive affect helps improve self-regulation following ego depletion. *Journal of Experimental Social Psychology 43(3)*. Doi: https://doi.org/10.1016/j.jesp.2006.05.007

*Chapter 3*

# Night Owls vs. Morning Larks

We all know individuals who perform or feel better in the morning, and others who perform or feel better at night. If you're reading this book you most likely fall into the latter group. But did you know it was actually science that coined the term 'morning larks' for people who enjoy the early hours and 'night owls' for those who prefer the evening? Science also uses the term 'chronotype,' as in early, late and mixed, to characterize an individual's cycle of sleep and wakefulness during a 24-hour period.

As you shall discover in this chapter, the differences between larks and owls are far more than just cultural stereotypes. Scientific findings confirm the biological, psychological, emotional and behavioral differences between morning larks and night owls.

## Biological Differences

Night owls and morning larks differ biologically. Research indicates that the white matter in the brains of morning larks is structurally different from the white matter of night owls. In a study conducted in Germany, scientists used specialized imaging technology known as Diffusion Tensor Imaging to study the white matter of individuals with different chronotypes. The study looked at 16 larks, 23 owls, and 20 individuals whose sleep patterns fell between lark or night owl extremes. The images revealed significant differences between the night owl's white matter structure and the white matter of the other two types of participants.

The circadian rhythm is also different between owls and larks. The circadian rhythm is a biological function driven by hormonal cycles that control our urges for sleep or wakefulness. Australian researchers recruited a group of psychology students from which they selected 22 participants who were at opposite ends of the chronotype spectrum. The participants remained in a bed for 27 hours without access to a clock. The evidence showed that evening chronotypes experienced melatonin levels and body temperature changes at different times than their morning lark counterparts even when participants found themselves in similar circumstances.

Another group of researchers observed that the night owl's biology (production of melatonin, cortisol, and body temperature) clashed with society's schedule. As a result, the night owl tries to conform to society's schedule during the week but is exhausted and reverts to a more natural pattern on days off, a pattern that these research-ers named "social jetlag."

## Psychological Differences

In addition to biological differences, night owls and morning larks differ psychologically. Research has shown a link between night owls and high intelligence. Researchers Satoshi Kanazawa and Kaja Perina used information from the National Longitudinal Study of Adolescent Health in the United States. The data strongly indicated that the smarter a person was, the later the individual's bed time would be. Other studies came to similar conclusions, finding that medical students and MBA students who were late chronotypes typically had higher IQs than their peers.

A higher IQ may not be the only advantage a night owl has. Other studies have linked late chronotypes to heightened creativity. One study looked at the sleep habits of a group of visual arts students and compared those habits to the sleep patterns of undergraduate students with different majors. The art students had both higher creativity and later chronotypes than their peers in other majors.

## Emotional Differences

Night owls and morning larks differ emotionally as well. According to Brazilian researchers, who gathered data on 200 volunteers ranging in age from 18 to 99, evening chronotypes have a much higher risk of experiencing depression. A team of British psychologists wanted to find out if late chronotypes were more likely to interpret facial expressions as being sad, which is a negative emotional bias found in people with acute depression. The researchers collected information from 226 people, including information on sleep patterns and measures of depression. The individuals also had to view photos of human faces and determine how sad each face looked. The participants with later chronotypes recognized sadness at a higher rate than other chronotypes.

Anxiety may also be more common for night owls. In one study conducted in the Netherlands, data was collected from nearly 2,000 participants. Of these participants, 676 were depressed or anxious. After comparing the participants' chronotypes, researchers found a correlation between anxiety and a late chronotype.

Interestingly, night owls seem better able to live in the present. When researchers Taciano Milfont and Miriam Schwarzenthal surveyed 142 students from New Zealand, they found that morning larks tend to focus on the future whereas night owls are more present-oriented. However, they also found that night owls tend to have "less emotional control" than mornings larks. In an internet survey, over six thousand participants answered questions about their emotional profile and their sleep patterns. Those with later chronotypes tended to be less emotionally adaptive.

**Behavioral Differences**

Lastly, night owls and morning larks demonstrate different behavioral tendencies. Night owls seem to remain mentally alert for longer periods of time than morning larks. Researchers used a group of people equally divided between late and early chronotypes and placed them on a fixed schedule to replicate a normal work day. Next, the researchers put the participants through a 36 hour test of alertness. The late chronotypes were able to maintain optimal alertness even when early chronotypes could not.

However, the social jetlag that night owls experience may also be linked to negative behaviors. In the study that coined the term 'social jetlag,' 501 participants volunteered information, and, those who were late chronotypes tended to consume more substances like caffeine, nicotine and alcohol. Night owls may also be more impulsive risk takers. In a sampling of 129 males, late chronotypes enjoyed novelty and were more willing to try new things in an impulsive manner. On the other hand, morning chronotypes were not novelty seekers and were more risk-averse.

While some research does point out negative traits of the night owls, the night owls amongst us should not be discouraged – after all, science shows that night owls may well be smarter and more creative than morning larks, as well as more present and alert. Additionally, there is evidence that if night owls are able to adjust daily schedules to their own circadian rhythms, they can maximize strengths and minimize weaknesses. In at least one study, arranging workers' schedules to better coincide with their circadian rhythm improved their sleep quality and well-being. Thus, if night owls can adjust their schedules, they may feel better and be better able to leverage their strengths against the early rising morning larks.

With this, we conclude our two chapter overview of the scientific data confirming the importance of a high quality morning routine and the native differences between owls and larks. In the following chapter, we will introduce the building blocks of a perfect morning routine for night owls along with the understanding that there is no 'one-size-fits-all' when it comes to morning rituals. Everyone is different. Rest assured, however, that by the end of this book you will know how to combine those building blocks to design your own ideal morning schedule.

## Resources

Antypa, N., Vogelzangs, N., Meesters, Y., Schoevers, R., & Penninx, B. (2015, September 14). Chronotype associations with depression and anxiety disorders in a large cohort study. *Depression and Anxiety.* Doi: https://doi.org/10.1002/da.22422.

Bhatti, U., Ahmadani, R., & Chohan, M. (2017, November). Intelligent Quotient (IQ) Comparison between Night Owls and Morning Larks Chronotypes in Medical Students. *Medical Forum*, 28(11): 29-32.

Caci, H., Robert, P., Boyer, P. (2004) Novelty seekers and impulsive subjects are low in morningness. *European Psychiatry*, 19, 79–84.

Hidalgo, M., Caumo, W., Posser, M., Coccaro, S., Camozzato, A., Chaves, M. (2009, May 14). Relationship between depressive mood and chronotype in healthy subject. *Psychiatry and Clinical Neurosciences*, 63(3) Doi: https://doi.org/

10.1111/j.1440-1819.2009.01965.x.

Horne, C., Marr-Phillips, S., Jawaid, R., Gibson, E., & Norbury, R. (2016, September 26). Negative emotional biases in late chronotypes. *Biological Rhythm Research*, 48(1). Doi: https://doi.org/10.1080/09291016.2016.1236461.

Kanazawa, S. & Perina, K. (2009). Why night owls are more intelligent. *Personality and Individual Differences*, 47(4), 685-690.

Lack, L., Bailey, M., Lovato, N., & Wright, H. (2009). Chronotype differences in circadian rhythms of temperature, melatonin, and sleepiness as measured in a modified constant routine protocol. *Nature and science of sleep*, 1: 1–8. Doi: 10.2147/NSS.S6234.

Milfont, T., & Schwarzenthal, M. (2014, January 7). Explaining why larks are future-oriented and owls are present-oriented: Self-control mediates the chronotype-time perspective relationship. *Chronobiology International*, 31(4). Doi:

https://doi.org/10.3109/07420528.2013.876428.

Ottoni, G., Antoniollo, E., & Lara, D. (2012, June 27). Circadian Preference is associated with emotional and affective temperaments. *Chronobiology International*, 29 (6): 786-793. Doi: https://doi.org/10.3109/07420528.2012.679329.

Piffer, D., Ponzi, D., Sapienza, P., Zingales, L., & Maestripieri, D. (2014, December). Morningness-eveningness and intelligence among high-achieving US students: Night owls have higher GMAT scores that early morning types in a top-ranked MBA program. *Intelligence*, 47: 107-112. Doi: https://doi.org/10.1016/j.intell.2014.09.009.

Ram-Vlasov, N., Tzischinsky, O., Green, A., & Shochat, T. (2016). Creativity and habitual sleep patterns among art and social sciences undergraduate students. *Psychology of Aesthetics, Creativity, and the Arts, 10*(3), 270-277. http://dx.doi.org/10.1037/aca0000062.

Rosenberg, J., Maximov, I., Reske, M., Grinberg, F., & Shah, N. (2014, January 1). "Early to bed, early to rise": Diffusion Tensor imaging identifies chronotype-specificity. *NeuroImage, 84,* 428-434. Doi: https://www.sciencedirect.com/science/article/pii/S105381191300921X.

Taillard, J., Philip, P., Claustrat, B., Capelli, A., Coste, O., Chaumet, G., Sagaspe, P. (2011, July 28). Time course of neurobehavioral alertness during extended wakefulness is morning- and evening-type healthy sleepers. *Chronobiology International,* 28(6). https://doi.org/10.3109/07420528.2011.590623.

Vetter, C., Fischer, D., Matera, J., & Roenneberg, T. (2015, March 30). Aligning work and circadian time in shift workers improves sleep and reduces circadian disruption. *Current Biology,* 25(7): 907-911. https://doi.org/10.1016/j.cub.2015.01.064.

Wittman, M., Dinich, J., Merrow, M., & Roenneberg, T. (2009, July 7). Social Jetlag:

Misalignment of Biological and Social Time. *Chronobiology International*, 23 (1-2). Doi: https://doi.org/10.1080/07420520500545979.

*Chapter 4*

# The Rule Of Six For A Perfect Morning Routine

Having experimented with my personal morning routine over time, and having assisted quite a few people in perfecting their own routines, I have discovered the Rule of Six for designing the perfect morning ritual. Before we take at look at the Rule of Six, let us set a few ground rules.

By 'morning,' let us be clear that the morning refers to the time after you get up, specifically, the first approximately two hours of your day, which could occur at any time of day or night, depending on your unique schedule. If you are like most night owls or work the late shift, your 'morning' might well be the afternoon. And this is of no significance whatsoever to the effectiveness of this technique. We are not trying to change your night owl proclivities, much less have you exclude yourself because you work nights.

The Rule of Six will benefit everyone, including early birds who are tired of the wham bam thank you ma'am, high speed morning ritual typically proffered. If you desire a more holistic and organic daytime routine then you are in the right place no matter the status of your circadian rhythms.

The usual recommendations for the morning ritual favor just getting it done as if you're a machine where 'doing it' is all that really matters, rather than seeking a meaningful experience in your wake-up ritual. The Rule of Six provides not only the quantity but also the quality of experience that is essential for a genuinely fulfilling morning wake-up and an effortlessly successful day.

These are the six simple elements or building blocks of a complete wake-up routine that will integrate and accelerate your entire life: organizing, inspiring, goal-setting, meditating, exercising and dressing. Eating, which we consider an optional part of your morning routine, would be a seventh segment if you choose to eat breakfast.

## Easy Organizing
This refers to the first and, invariably, sleepiest part of your daytime routine. It consists of sleepwalking through personal ablutions, performing a groggy household 'reset' while making that first cup of coffee or tea and begrudgingly checking emails.

## Easy Inspiration
The second part of your routine involves setting the proper mindset for your day while having your second morning beverage. I call this the Mindset Formula. It consists of raising your

energy through positive focus followed by inspirational reading and goal-setting. Because goal-setting involves learning a new technique, I have made it the next essential step in your routine.

### Easy Goal-setting

In the third step in your morning ritual, and as a continuation of the Mindset Formula, you will learn how to quickly build a series of positive habits that will transform your life.

### Easy Meditation

Here we allow ourselves to rest in the silence and sense our oneness with the Invisible (otherwise known as the Field, the Source or God). We also explore the value of other types of meditation such as visualization meditation, contemplative meditation and mantra meditation.

## Easy Exercise

Beginning with easy movements and gentle stretches, this segment will tune up and energize you without requiring any willpower.

## Easy Dressing

It's natural to want to shower and dress after exercise. Therefore, you will find it an easy and effortless flow to make getting dressed the sixth step in your routine.

## Easy Eating

If you tend to be hungry in the early part of your day or are facing a long delay before you can have lunch, then after exercise or after getting dressed would be the perfect time to have a healthy breakfast designed to satisfy and energize as the seventh, although optional, step in your morning routine.

Later on in this book, we will delve into both the obvious and the hidden or higher meaning, purpose and value of each of these elements, how to select, design and construct your personalized morning routine from these elements or add your own, and how to install the habits needed to easily carry them out.

In the next chapter, we will explore why organizing is the first step in a balanced morning routine. Be prepared to discover how doing your organizing first provides multiple long-lasting benefits for your body, mind and spirit!

*Chapter 5*

# Easy Organizing

Organizing is a means of setting a fresh stage for the activities that will ensue in your new day. I prefer to call it a mindful morning reset, where any disarray in your environment that has carried over from yesterday is consciously put back in place before you begin your today.

You may prefer to do the reset in the late evening, but consider that if you have had a busy day and are eager to relax, then doing an evening reset could feel too effortful. In addition, there are late day activities that you already perform, such as checking the doors and the alarm, closing curtains, shutting or opening windows, shutting down the lights, bringing out the trash, clearing clutter from the main living area, helping your kids get ready for bed, doing your evening ablutions, etc. For this reason, I recommend the mindful morning reset, which helps to distribute household chores more evenly.

## The Ins and Outs of a Mindful Morning Reset

The mindful morning reset begins with your usual morning hygiene such as washing your face, rinsing with mouthwash and/or brushing your teeth and, for reasons we will cover later, changing out of your night clothes into comfortable 'exercise' clothes. It then continues with giving your full attention (mindfulness) to your home environment and re-ordering anything out of place. Many of these things you already do naturally, activities such as opening the curtains, opening the windows, making your bed, putting away items that should be stored, collecting cups and glasses, checking and restocking paper goods in kitchen and bathrooms, wiping down bathroom mirrors, emptying all small wastebaskets into a primary container for later disposal, emptying the dishwasher, loading the dishwasher, making coffee, turning on lights, plumping decorative pillows, watering plants, etc.

As time-consuming as the above sounds, the morning reset need only occupy the first five to 20 minutes of your day, depending on the size of your home and household, and the amount of your household help.

Once the reset has been completed, it's time to sit down with your morning beverage and phone to check your emails and texts. This is done to relieve your mind of concerns about emergency business or personal matters. While viewing my messages I also perform triage, meaning I delete, file, leave in my inbox for later, or respond if absolutely necessary. In my experience, if you don't check your messages, it may distract you from investing fully in the steps that come next in your morning routine. Checking your phone should take no more than 5 or 10 minutes.

## The Higher Meaning of a Morning Reset

While the above addresses seemingly mundane actions of everyday life, there is a higher psychological, symbolic and spiritual significance to everything you do which must not be overlooked if you are to understand why each part of a morning routine is important. For example, practicing mindfulness while creating order in your home environment at the start of the day not only accomplishes practical and necessary housekeeping, but it also helps you feel mentally 'in order.' It brings you into the present moment so that you may live more fully in the 'now,' free of yesterday's residue. Furthermore, it clears the mind and opens room for new ideas. On an even deeper level, doing a morning reset also helps encourage an unhindered connection to your higher self and to the gifts it bestows.

As a night owl, you are likely objecting strongly at this point to having to be so 'active' right out of the box. 'I can barely make it into the kitchen to start coffee,' I hear you cry, 'much less do housekeeping.' But please recognize that we are talking about a series of minor, physical tasks, all performed while you move at your own pace through your home. It should never feel intense or excessive, nor should it be done more quickly than is comfortable. In the process of moving gently about, reordering your home, you not only achieve the spiritual uplift of creating order for a new day, but you also increase the energy flow in your physical body and set the stage for an active day.

Let me add here a small but important efficiency tip. When doing your morning reset, always begin where you are by putting your attention on your immediate surroundings. Then take care of all tasks in your immediate area before you move on to the next. If you do not consciously focus on what needs to be done in your immediate vicinity, you are likely to end up moving around the house at random, doing your clean-up while your mind is on other things. This defeats the purpose of a morning reset, which is to encourage you to begin the day in a mindful way. It also increases the length of time you spend on the tasks and prevents you from creating an efficient system. Therefore, aim to consolidate your movements, as opposed, for example, to increasing them in order to have a larger step count for the sake of exercise. In so doing, you make the morning reset as quick and easy as possible. In addition, by putting your attention on the task you will automatically find ways to streamline and shorten the job even further over time.

You have begun to raise your energy for the new day by taking care of morning hygiene, refreshing your environment through the gentle movements of a household reset, and checking your phone. In the next chapter, we will explore the second phase of your morning routine, which addresses your mindset by focusing, inspiring and uplifting your mind.

*Chapter 6*

# Easy Inspiration

No morning routine would be complete without an inspirational segment, meaning a practice that uplifts your mind, enhances clarity about your goals and sets positive expectations. I recommend three techniques for this portion of your wake-up schedule: the mental reset, inspirational or wisdom reading and my 'train your brain' goal-setting. We will look at them one at a time.

**Mental Reset**

This is where you settle down with your coffee in your favorite spot on the sofa within reaching distance of a notebook, and begin to jot down several things you feel happy about. But don't just come up with things at the 'head' level, as if you're a school kid trying to please the teacher. The point is to make this exercise real.

Try to find at least three new things that you feel happy about, making an effort to think back to the previous day if necessary. This may include what you are grateful for, relieved about or something that you enjoyed doing.

For each item, sense your heart chakra, meaning put your attention on the center of your chest for the feeling of happiness when you are thinking about what you are happy about. The feeling of happiness may include anything from the mildest movement of energy in your heart area to a sense of utter and complete joy. If something comes to mind that brings a sensation of relief or gratitude, it may feel more like a sinking deep into your heart with a subtle or not so subtle urge to cry. Don't be afraid of these feelings. Just stay with the sensations in your heart chakra (heart area).

When you grab your notebook to write down these items, don't belabor it. It should take literally seconds to jot the three items down, for example: call from A, sunset last night, thanks from X client.

Part two of the Mental Reset is as follows: jot down three actions above and beyond your everyday activities that would truly add joy to your day. Big or small, these things must be under your control. In other words, they should not depend on someone else doing something for you or behaving in a certain way, nor should they involve fantasy or wishful thinking. They should be actions that are within your power to take, such that if you do take them it will enhance your life somehow, for example: buy present for R, ride bike, be patient with E. no matter what.

Again, jotting down these items should take literally seconds. Now you are ready for part two of the Inspiration segment.

**Inspirational Reading**

This is where I reach for my Kindle and fire up the Tao Te Ching. For the past several months, every day begins with reading a few chapters. If you haven't read the Tao Te Ching, a chapter is like a small poem, though more substantial than a haiku. I read two or three of these chapters each morning and ponder their meaning. Whenever I finish the book, which has 80 plus chapters, I start over. But that's just me. I also spend time reading portions from one or two other inspirational, spiritual, religious, literary or educational books by the writers I trust. It often isn't so much what is said as the positive effect of being in contact with a highly intelligent, spiritual mind and the resultant 'food for thought.' Also, in this way I both consume the material that matters to me and include reading books in my busy, daily schedule.

Have you wanted to read the entire Bible or the collected works of Shakespeare, but never seem to find the time? This is where you can delve into these brilliant resources or whatever uplifts your spirit on a daily basis, and reap the benefits.

By reminding yourself daily of what you are happy about, what would make your day even better, and then spending as much time as possible, but at least 15 or 20 minutes, with elevating, educational or uplifting reading, you are raising your vibration to a higher level. What does that mean exactly? Your vibrational frequency is your energetic signature and reflects your mental and spiritual state. A higher frequency means better health, clearer mind and a more positive life experience. The higher the frequency the better. For this reason, in the morning we aim to raise our frequency and thereby reap the rewards of a positive mindset.

In the next chapter, we will explore goal-setting, the third part of the Mindset Formula. We gave this step its own chapter because of its immense value. When properly and consistently applied, our goal-setting technique will allow you to consciously redesign and transform your entire life.

# Chapter 7

# Easy Goal-Setting

No mental reset portion of a morning routine is complete without goal-setting. However, the kind of goal-setting I recommend is a method I discovered that has fast-acting and long-lasting results. I call this technique Train Your Brain. In the context of this book, where we are building a morning routine for night owls that will ease you into action in your new day, the Train Your Brain technique will be focused on helping you quickly and easily perform the steps in your morning routine. Once you master the morning routine, you can apply the technique to any other goals you wish to set in your daily life.

Train Your Brain ultimately provides a means of creating a perfect life by adding or subtracting habits and patterns from your everyday life, that in so doing will automatically result in your having the experience of your perfect lifestyle and, ultimately, your perfect life. Train Your Brain shows you how to live one complete and fulfilling day after another. By perfecting your days, one day at a time, you effortlessly construct your magnificent life.

The success industry typically focuses on the big picture and the long game whereas life is lived in the moment by moment experience of being. For example, we may think we want to be rich and famous, and lust after methods to achieve those dreams, but our lives are ultimately the cumulative experience of living here and now. The life well-lived is in every way as much a testament to your greatness as is public recognition and reward for something you achieve. How many so-called successful people have neglected their health or their family, created unwholesome and imbalanced habits, or compromised themselves in other ways while pursuing their dream? How many others never break free of the stultifying habits and patterns passed on through generations that cause a 'walking dead' existence devoid of passion and creativity?

Living well is an art and begins with mastering your day. Live a beautiful day and tomorrow has the potential to be even better. Live one beautiful day after another and you will automatically fulfill your potential, guaranteed! And in the process, you will retain your health, your happiness, your balance and your authenticity.

So how do we Train Your Brain to effortlessly carry out the steps of your morning routine? It begins with creating a list of the steps of your morning routine. There are six steps in our program, although your unique routine may have more or less steps. We will be showing you how to design your own personal morning routine later in this book, but for now, let us use these six steps as our focus. The steps are as follows:

Step One: Organize

    A) Personal Hygiene

    B) Household Reset

    C) Check email and texts

Step Two: Inspiration

    A) Mental Reset

    B) Inspirational Reading

Step Three: Goal-setting

Step Four: Meditation

Step Five: Exercise

Step Six: Get Dressed

Step Seven (optional): Eat Breakfast

## Morning Routine Trial Run

We suggest starting with a Morning Routine Trial Run. This means that you make the decision to jump right in and perform our recommended morning routine, or your own variation, as soon as possible. The purpose of this trial run is to establish a base line for determining the steps you are comfortable with and the steps you are resistant to or find reason to skip altogether. Each person varies in regard to which steps will require brain training right away. Often, brain training will also be needed down the road, for even when a step may seem comfortable at first, resistance to a particular step or sub-step can build over time.

While going through the various parts of the morning routine, notice if you feel resistance when thinking about, initiating or performing a particular step, or if you actually procrastinate or skip doing it altogether. Whether it is your first time taking that step or your hundredth, you will need to apply the Train Your Brain technique to it. Some of the steps will not require any brain training whatsoever, as they will be easy, enjoyable and/or automatic for you. You are likely doing some or many of these things already. But others will require applying the Train Your Brain technique in order to program them into your schedule.

**Train Your Brain**

So what is the Train Your Brain technique? You will need a notebook and a pen for this exercise. From the list above, determine which step or sub-step you are avoiding or feel resistance to doing then answer the questions What, When, Where and Why, and write down your answers. For example:

What: Household reset

When: Everyday, starting tomorrow, Dec. 4th, after personal hygiene

Where: My home

Why: To create order in my environment before I start my day.

Then write a composite statement. 'Brain, have me effortlessly do a household reset after personal hygiene, starting tomorrow, December 4th.' Say that sentence aloud three times, with intentionality and clarity, as if you are talking directly to your brain. Yes, imagine that you are talking to your brain! You will also need to repeat the statement aloud in the same way three times before bedtime.

In creating your statement, be sure to always associate the step you are building in with the step that precedes it so that when you perform the step that precedes it, it will automatically trigger the thought to do the next step, which is the one you are building in.

Following our example above – doing a household reset after personal hygiene – the next morning you will notice the thought comes to do the household reset after you do your personal hygiene. Even if you still feel intense resistance, say to yourself 'I will put one thing away.' Then do so. The idea is to perform a 'placeholder' act that will start to install the new habit. By associating it with 'after personal hygiene,' you anchor the act.

Repeat the instruction to your brain again three times during your morning routine and three times before bedtime. If resistance persists, tell yourself you'll just spend a minute or two minutes, etc., on the household reset. Make it feel easy, and then perform the placeholder act. Once you have taken action to do even one thing, you are likely to continue and complete the household reset. If not, no problem. By continuing to repeat brain instructions morning and night and doing placeholder acts as long as resistance persists, in short order you will find yourself performing a full household reset.

Proceed to do the same thing with each resistant or skipped step in the routine. Create a Brain Instruction, write it down, repeat it three times with energy and clarity while imagining you are talking to your own brain, and then do this again before bedtime. Soon you will install each step in your brain, which will cause you to do it automatically But don't forget to associate it with a previous step in your brain instruction, such as "Brain, have me meditate after I set my goals."

That is all there is to it. However, I usually recommend making your first brain instruction about following brain instructions, such as:

What: Give brain instructions

When: Everyday, starting tomorrow (state date) after inspirational reading

Where: My living room

Why: To train my brain by building in the habit of giving brain instructions.

Then write the brain instruction statement: "Brain, have me date and write down my brain instructions after the inspirational reading portion of my morning routine, and have me say them aloud three times then and three times before bed."

Important tip: If you resist repeating your brain instructions at night, be sure to create a separate brain instruction for that as well.

You don't have to wait for your morning routine to add a new brain instruction. A good time to add a brain instruction for the next step in your morning routine is before bed. Then repeat it in the morning during the goal-setting portion of your morning ritual. You may be working on more than one step, so make sure to also repeat any other brain instructions you have previously set, both in the morning and again before bed.

Automating all parts of your morning routine may take only a few days for some steps while others may take up to several weeks, so be patient with yourself as you go through this process. When all the steps in your routine are literally automatic, easy to perform and without resistance you may then stop working on them and start building into your day new goals if you so desire. But please don't focus off of the morning routine steps until the entire structure is in place and feels automatic.

With this technique in hand the world is literally your oyster. In addition to the perfect morning routine, you can set up your ideal lifestyle and quickly be living it. No matter how resistant you may have been in the past, you will now do those things that you knew were right for you but seemingly lacked the will to accomplish.

In the next chapter, we will introduce meditation to your morning routine, explore various kinds of meditation and discover why it is important to meditate every day.

## Chapter 8

# Easy Meditation

Meditation has more benefits than any other activity you can perform in your morning routine. Whether you desire to open a portal to a higher state of consciousness, quiet your mind, center yourself, lower stress, heal stress-related health issues, find a solution to a problem or visualize an alternate reality, meditation is the way.

Once you have raised your vibration through positive thoughts, inspirational reading, and goal-setting in the mindset portion of your morning routine, you are ready for meditation.

The question is, what kind of meditation do you want to pursue? The beauty of the morning routine is its flexibility, not the least of which is the nature of your meditation. Start with one technique and then add or alternate with others as desired.

Basic meditation aims to quiet the mind. Most of the people in our culture are lurching around like 'drunken monkeys,' to quote the great Russian philosopher Georges Gurdjieff, their minds filled with constant chatter. Is your mind filled with thoughts, ideas and judgments about things happening or not happening in your life now? Are you dwelling on things you experienced in the past that caused you emotional pain? Or perhaps you are worried about the future and can't see your way out.

These are all common mental activities of what is considered a normal human being. Be that as it may, the truth is, this sort of mental activity is not common in those in more advanced states of consciousness because it does not support connecting with one's higher self, accessing higher knowledge and creativity, and fulfilling one's true purpose.

By quieting your mind, you have an opportunity to raise your consciousness to a higher level and in so doing recalibrate your entire existence on planet Earth. Vibration is a frequency, not unlike the different channels on your television set where each new channel or, in this case, each new frequency, brings a different experience. Just as certain shows on television offer much higher quality than others, if you raise your frequency your reality upgrades instantly just as if you changed the channel on the television set to a higher quality show.

That is a big promise for such a simple act as sitting in silence and aiming to quiet your mind. But it is the long term result of daily meditation. On the other hand, your meditation time can be used to pose questions and receive answers from your higher self or to visualize a desired outcome in your attempt to manifest a new reality. Meditation can also be an opportunity to mentally repeat a special mantra, which is a positive phrase or word that contains a quality you wish to embody or something you wish to bring into your life.

There is nothing wrong with trying all the different kinds of meditation and picking and choosing from among them according to your need. But the highest use of meditation is to quiet the mind and allow yourself to sense your core identity as The I Am, the Creative Essence of all that is, which is sometimes referred to as The Field if you are scientifically oriented, or as God, Source, Infinite Being if spiritually oriented. Reconnecting with your true self may lead to healing, inspiration, solving seemingly insoluble problems, discovering your exceptional abilities and accessing higher dimensional knowledge.

Silence is the healer, so find a quiet place for your meditation. Going quiet internally, with your mind poised in 'the void,' allows for a total mental rest and reset. This begins by sitting with straight back, feet on floor, hands resting on upper legs, palms down and simply aiming to quiet your mind. Try this now. Close your eyes and sit in the silence. Don't judge the thoughts that continue to arise. Allow your thoughts to pass across the screen of your mind without having to inspect, attach or follow them. After a period of time, you may reach a point where thought stops altogether. That is where you rest in the void and allow yourself to be healed. Do not expect fanfare, bells and whistles.

Healing takes place when you remove yourself from the fray and align with your true inner self. That Infinite, Unlimited part of you is always there in the background, awaiting your attention to It. Here is the secret: do not expect It to seek you out, for It never emerges from the background to assert Its presence and demand your attention. You must come into the realization of It. Until you are able to recognize and consciously align with It, it is as if that part of you does not exist. And for most of the people in this world, It does not exist nor is what is being written in this paragraph believable if you cannot comprehend how you are an extension of Infinite Being.

No matter, for meditation serves us without judgment or discrimination. It meets us exactly where we are at, takes whatever we bring, and gives whatever we need. So go with confidence into your meditation and enjoy the adventure of floating inside your own Being.

In the following chapter, we shall take a look at why exercise is critically important for your morning routine and how a night owl can actually enjoy exercising in the morning even if you would never dare lift a toe before sunset!

## Chapter 9

# Easy Exercise

For a night owl, the secret of enjoying morning exercise begins with understanding its higher meaning. What, you say, exercise means something besides increasing heart rate, burning calories and building muscle? Absolutely. There is a deeper significance to exercise as well as to everything else you do. By deliberately increasing energy through movement and breath, you automatically alter your vibrational frequency which in turn expands your consciousness, even if only to a slight degree.

Just a small shift in consciousness is enough to give you the new ideas, perspectives and inspiration that can result in an improved life experience. When you exercise consistently you, therefore, not only support greater physical well-being but also a state of mind that correlates with a higher quality of life. The power of exercise is accessed by starting with the gentlest of movements and then continues, as your energy gradually builds, and depending on how much time you have, to more physically demanding movements.

The perfect morning exercise for a night owl is Tai Chi, which in Chinese means Supreme Ultimate Exercise. If you've ever noticed a group of people, whether in television shows, movies or in real life, standing outdoors on the green, by the sea or in a park, and with deep concentration making slow head, arm and leg movements in unison, then you have witnessed the beauty of Tai Chi. I highly recommend purchasing a Tai Chi video from a site such as Amazon to help you learn this exquisite, gentle process of moving and raising energy throughout your entire body while simultaneously balancing and healing it.

But if a Tai Chi video is not available to you or if following it does not appeal to you, then I recommend using any technique that enables you to warm up by gently and slowly isolating and stretching your neck, shoulders, arms and spine for ten or fifteen minutes. Make sure your chosen workout feels easy and pleasant to you as your anticipation of a comfortable experience will encourage you to start it and stick with it. Night owls are not designed for intense morning exercise, so it's important to engage in comfortable and easy exercise that serves primarily as a warm-up.

**Suggested Stretching Sequence**

Take a standing position for these upper body and spinal stretches:

With arms at side - Five each of neck bends forward, then to the right, to the back and to the left.

With arms at side - Five neck rolls to the left and then five to the right.

With arms at side - Five each of right side shoulder lifts, shoulder rolls back and shoulder rolls forward.

With arms at side - Five each of left side shoulder lifts, shoulder rolls back and shoulder rolls forward.

With arms at side - Five simultaneous (both arms) shoulder lifts, shoulder rolls back and shoulder rolls forward.

Extend your right arm straight out to the right and your left arm to the left with thumbs turned forward and do ten forward arm rolls, meaning, make small circles with your arms.

Maintain arm position, but turn thumbs toward back and do ten backward arm rolls, again making small circles with your arms.

Repeat that sequence two to four more times.

Bend your right arm over your right shoulder and connect with your left hand behind your back and hold for 8 seconds.

Bend your left arm over your left shoulder and connect with your right hand behind your back and hold for 8 seconds.

With both arms behind your back at waist level, grasp your right arm at the wrist with your left hand and pull for a stretch, holding for 8 seconds. Repeat with the left arm.

Stretch your arms out in front of you, parallel to each other, and swing your arms all the way to the right and all the way to the left. Repeat five times.

Do 10 side bends, alternating left and right as follows: move your legs about 18 inches apart and stretch the left arm down the left leg while bending left as far as possible and curving the right arm over your head and holding for 8 seconds, and then switch to the right leg by moving right arm down right leg and bending right as far as possible while curving the left arm over your head and holding for 8 seconds. Repeat this sequence 5-10 times.

End the stretching series with five spine rolls where you stand with legs 12 inches apart, take a deep breath and hold, then raise your arms and drop your entire upper body down from the waist with knees slightly bent, hold for twelve seconds, then exhale while you rise up to the count of 10, and repeat.

The purpose of describing the above regimen is just to give you an idea of what you might do during the ten or fifteen minute stretching component of your exercise period. Remember at all times that the goal is to maintain a gentle and easy series of movements, completely avoiding strain. Probably you learned to do warm-up exercises like these and more in school, at the gym, before sports, or in a yoga, dance or acting class, but if you need more guidance, visit Amazon to check out their exercise videos. Whatever is easiest and appeals to you is the right thing for this portion of your exercise routine.

After that, if you have any type of cardio exercise equipment in your home such as a recumbent bike, which I use, or a treadmill, now is the time to do a short stint on the equipment at a comfortable pace. If not, then skip this part of the exercise routine and go on to the last segment.

The last part of my recommended exercise program involves getting on the floor and crawling for five minutes. Why crawling? Because I have found that crawling is the one exercise that is a tonic for all parts of the body but does not require a lot of effort or time to reap its benefits. Scientific studies have proven that crawling not only works out, strengthens and tones the whole body, but it also integrates and tunes up the brain itself to increase intelligence, memory and cognition, as well as improve mood and energy levels.

I was so excited about my own seemingly miraculous healing after discovering crawling several years ago, that I wrote an entire book about it entitled, *Lower Back Pain Relief: How to Cure Your Chronic Lower Back Pain in Only Ten Days*. The beauty of my book is that it not only explains in detail the scientific basis and specific procedure for using crawling to heal debilitating lower back pain but it also goes far beyond focusing on the lower back to reveal how you can use the miracle power of crawling to improve virtually every system and organ of the body! Check it out on Amazon. You can't go wrong including crawling in your daily regime and I highly recommend it. Just be sure to build up to five minutes over time as crawling can be taxing at first. Starting at thirty seconds is all you need to begin reaping great results.

In the next chapter, we will briefly tackle the final portion of your wake-up plan by learning the right approach to getting dressed, eating breakfast, and going forth heroically to conquer your day.

## Chapter10

# Conscious Showering, Dressing, Eating

Y ou've completed the exercise portion of your morning routine and now is the perfect time to take a shower and get dressed. Before you do so, consider that the higher meaning of cleansing your body is spiritual renewal. You not only freshen and hydrate your body by bathing but you also clear impurities from your aura, which is the invisible energy field that surrounds your physical body. The result is a new you; a refreshed, purified and healed being.

With this understanding of the higher meaning of bathing, recognize that you are performing a purification ritual whenever you bathe or even just wash your hands. You can go further by creating a concept for every phase of your shower that allows you to symbolically heal yourself. This is done by stating mentally, "I now clear all toxic energy from my aura" as you soap up and wash off under hot water. Other phrases that may be helpful include, "My entire body is made new with this cleansing," or "All my anger is washed away as I take this shower." The goal is to use the shower for more than its most conventional, surface purpose. Yes, that purpose will be accomplished, but so too can a higher purpose if you take a moment to program it that way.

Most people have long ago suppressed the imaginative, playful part of their being as a result of the relentless demands to conform by their family, their peers, their school and their work. Do you secretly long to feel the magic in everyday life like you did when you were a child? Guess what, that ability to transform ordinary experiences into something more potent is still available to you. No one need know how you frame your time in the shower, or how you think about any other activity that you wish to turn into a magical event. When we understand that we can use the power of our imagination to add an additional positive dimension to everyday experiences, we live artfully and with greater enjoyment of life.

**Getting Dressed**

Now that you have been born anew, it's time to select your clothing and get dressed. Before you do, take a moment to think about what colors you would enjoy wearing. While you may have restrictions on the type of clothing you can wear during the work week, there is always some room for creativity. The selection of color is highly significant as colors will enhance, detract or balance your energy. For example, red is a good choice when your energy is low as it is an energy enhancer. Blue on the other hand tends to create a more serene and controlled vibration. It's wise to wear blue when you feel stressed as it will balance your nervous energy. White gives a feeling of innocence and holiness. Wear white when you want to highlight your purity of being and good intentions.

Your reaction to various colors is likely to be a personal one, and that is a good reason to take a moment to sense within before you choose the colors of your wardrobe for the day. According to your need, try to select a color that enhances, balances or neutralizes; avoid drab, dull colors when you need to be uplifted, and so on.

Also make sure your clothing is clean, without wrinkles and without visible wear and tear. This includes the undergarments that will not be seen by others and are only known to you. All that you wear matters because everything you do has an effect on your vibration and your self esteem. At best, the right choice of clothing can elevate you. At worst, the wrong choice can subtly lower your vibration which may be deleterious to your optimal well-being.

The same may be said for your choice of fabrics and design. While fashion is not the purview of this book, we mention these matters of clothing style, condition, quality and color to raise your awareness of the importance of selecting clothing that makes you feel good about yourself and your choices, and that presents you to the world in the best possible way.

## Eating Breakfast

If, like me, you practice intermittent fasting, which involves waiting sixteen hours between your last meal of the previous day and your first meal of the new day, then your first meal will begin with lunch. But if you do plan to eat breakfast as part of your morning routine, now is the time. In either case, I can't encourage you enough to make the effort to research the best food choices for your lifestyle, body type and metabolism. I highly recommend exploring the wealth of information about diet on www.mercola.com which is an amazing resource for all matters of health.

**Mirror Work**

You've finished eating breakfast or skipped breakfast and are now dressed and ready to leave for work. Not only is it time to brush your teeth if you haven't yet done so, but you also have the perfect opportunity to do mirror work. This is a simple process of looking at yourself in the mirror and making a positive declaration.

So how do you choose what to declare? I suggest asking yourself what do you want more than anything else? Then turn the first thought that comes into your head into a positive affirmation. In a nutshell, a positive affirmation is a short statement, usually one sentence that begins with I am, I have, I do, or with another present tense verb. Fill in the blanks and you have your perfect affirmation. For example, "I now weigh 120 lbs." "I am fearless in making my presentations." "I meet my perfect mate." "I easily find the ideal new home." Just make sure it's something you truly want to experience in your life, and be careful not to place it in the future by using words such as 'I will.' Always make a present time statement of what you want as if you already have it.

If your heart's desire is for something that seems impossible or out of reach, instead of declaring for that thing, declare: I don't know how I (state desire), I only know I do so now (or, I have it now), and so it is.

That's mirror work in a nutshell. Just be sure to continue to repeat the same statement every time you look in the mirror until it finally takes shape in your reality. At that time, simply ask yourself again, 'What do I most want right now?' and then create a statement to reflect that new goal.

After performing this last phase of your morning routine, I promise that you will be so charged up and ready to conquer the world, nothing can stand in your way. By taking the time to create order in your home, express gratitude, install daily goals, read wisdom writings, meditate, exercise, purify, dress, nourish yourself healthfully and declare your heart's desire as so, you have powerfully invested in a greater you and are on your way to being the best that you can be.

That said, you may have certain preferences or considerations in structuring your morning routine, and we respect that. Therefore, we devoted the following chapter to helping you customize this process and design your own perfect morning routine.

*Chapter11*

# Designing Your Own Routine

D o you find yourself taking issue with the demands of a morning routine? After all, you barely have enough time to get through your usual preparations for work, so how could you possibly sit and meditate or do even half the steps of a full-scale morning ritual?

Or perhaps you don't need to do certain of the tasks, like the household reset. You're one of the lucky ones who has someone else doing those chores for you. Or maybe you just don't like the idea of certain of the steps, like reading books or setting up and issuing brain instructions.

Fellow night owls, I completely understand how challenging it may seem to add anything new to your existing morning schedule. It takes all your strength and willpower just to wake with the alarm, get ready for work and head out the door. How on earth are you going to perform the various steps of a perfect morning routine?

Don't worry, we've got your back. In this chapter, we're going to let you off the hook. Consider designing both a short routine and a full routine. Whenever time is at a premium, the modified or short routine will suffice so long as it contains the primary ingredients of a powerful morning ritual: meditation and gentle exercise, as well as a mindful approach to getting dressed and eating breakfast. The time spent on the household reset and the mental reset steps of gratitude, inspirational reading and goal-setting can be adjusted to suit your needs on those days when every minute counts.

However, please know that you will be losing the full power of the morning routine if this becomes your regular practice. The complete routine must be performed as often as possible -- at the very minimum on the weekends -- in order to receive the benefits of a wake-up ritual. Furthermore, without regular practice, turning your new morning routine into a habit becomes increasingly difficult. What that means is that any part of the routine that feels foreign and/or effortful will never become automatic unless there is a concerted effort to repeat the routine daily with as few breaks in the pattern as possible.

If you dislike any part of the recommended routine and are considering eliminating it, we suggest first creating a placeholder action. What that means is simply making one move in the direction of performing that step before going on to the next step. By not eliminating the step completely and doing a little something, i.e., making a gesture in the direction of performing the act, you are more likely to overcome your resistance to that task and will eventually be able to carry out the full step with ease. This leverages both the Gestalt principle of closure and the theory of inertia from the laws of physics. Gestalt therapy research tells us that the brain seeks closure. Once we begin something, we seek to complete it. The laws of physics tell us that once we overcome inertia by taking even the smallest action, we create momentum which energizes the next action, and the next.

Finally, you may already have your favorite practices for meditation, exercise or for one or more of the mental reset steps of expressing gratitude, inspirational reading and goal-setting, and would like to substitute your preferred practices for the ones we recommend. Our advice here is to first give our recommended method a try. Once you have a handle on how it feels to practice the morning routine our way, and experience the results it brings, you can make an informed decision as to whether your technique works equally well as ours or is better for you than ours. If you should decide to integrate one of your preferred practices, you may do so as long as it duplicates the primary objective of that step in the morning routine and results in raised energy and a positive mindset.

In the next chapter, we will examine another issue that is likely to arise eventually when carrying out a morning routine, which is whether or not you should, on a given morning, over-throw your established routine in favor of a strong impulse to do something else. In other words, we will answer the question of when, if ever, should following the inspiration and motivation of the moment trump your morning routine.

*Chapter12*

# Habit vs. Flow

The longer you engage in the practice of an early day ritual, the more likely you will experience a morning when an urge arises to do something else in place of your morning routine. In that moment, you are faced with a quandary about whether or not you should act on the impulse or suppress it and go through with your usual routine.

My students and I have regularly dealt with that issue and, as a result, I have developed a protocol for best practices. But before we review it, it would be wise to understand the difference between habit and flow, in what ways those two seemingly opposite states are interrelated, and how both have a specific area of vulnerability. Once understood, the answer becomes obvious.

Habit is defined here as an act that is performed automatically with no or little thought or sense of effort involved. The beauty of habits is that they allow the many necessary, repetitive activities of everyday life to be accomplished with little conscious effort, leaving us with available energy for more demanding pursuits.

Consider that when you start life as an infant, you have no developed habits and no understanding of how anything is done. Imagine if that state of mind never left you. Doing the simplest things of everyday life would dominate your day as you struggled with remembering to do those things at all, much less when, where, why and how to do them!

Automaticity is a gift from your brain which deserves to be recognized and treated with respect. It is a dispensation that allows you to develop your potential far beyond the minimal survival skills needed to get through a day. Therefore, habit should not be denigrated as it often is when judged as facilitating mindless, unimportant tasks. Just imagine if you had a brain injury that caused you to forget how to brush your teeth or even why or when to brush your teeth, or that caused you to stand at a streetlight while cars zoomed by, not remembering to press the walk button. Imagine if you forgot how to drive, how to turn on the TV or your other electronic devices, how to dress yourself, cook, how to tie shoelaces or button a shirt, etc. Mastering these tasks and trying to make them into habits would take over your life.

Flow, on the other hand, is a brain state associated with inspiration, creativity, ease of performance and deep concentration. This is the pearl of great price sought by creative minds in the arts and sciences from the beginning of time. Many blocked writers and other creative individuals have been known to turn to alcohol or drugs to release inhibitions and expand awareness in hopes of enabling the experience of creative flow. The flow state is revered as signaling surrender to higher mind which can issue forth original thought and effortless creativity.

Also called 'being in the zone,' flow can empower players to win a World Series or transport a marathon runner across the finish line long after their raw energy runs out. Without flow, many of the greatest accomplishments of western civilization would never have been achieved.

We also talk about being 'in the flow,' meaning that we're in the right place at the right time doing the right thing; everything feels easy and harmonious.

On the surface, the enjoyable sensation of being in the flow appears to be the opposite of the demands and strictures of a morning ritual, causing the two to potentially be at war. So why should we pair habit with flow rather than against it; in what way are they interrelated?

I posit that habit is a morphed form of flow, meaning that habit is flow as applied to a single, isolated task. Habit possesses the effortlessness, mindlessness and super-competence of the flow state, and, depending on the nature of the task, also has the potential for eliciting higher creativity and access to higher mind. In the right context, habit can set the stage for entering the pure flow state, with its inspiration, creative breakthroughs, deep focus, loss of time, enhanced performance ability and exalted emotions.

The question is what happens when your early day energy appears to flow in a different direction than toward the stacked habits of your morning routine? For example, if you're an artist, one morning you may get a strong urge to paint at the time of your morning routine, which is possibly hours before your scheduled painting time. Do you give in to the compelling urge or do you ignore it and force yourself through the morning routine?

While each situation needs to be evaluated on its own terms, in general, it is best to stick with the habits of the morning routine, and here is why. Habits are not easy to build. If they are new or initially uncomfortable, they tend to dissipate rapidly with neglect. For this reason, you ignore your morning routine at your own peril. What may begin as an atypical departure from your morning routine in order to follow a compelling urge or inspiration can become instantly addictive if not held in check, leading to doing it again. In short order, the voices of procrastination and resistance reappear and cause you to permanently fall 'off the wagon' where your morning routine is no more and all of its benefits denigrated by a part of your mind that attempts to justify its rebellion. The inevitable result is that after an initial 'high' you will eventually find yourself feeling unmoored and in a lower state than when you first began to work on your morning routine.

Why is this? It's because your morning routine is a powerful personal development tool that should not be treated lightly. It deserves every respect and to be honored with regular use. The different parts of the routine build up a state of consciousness that enhances who you were prior to engaging with this process. By giving in even once to a contradictory urge, you leave yourself vulnerable to the inner voices that would stand in the way of your continued advancement, while providing you with the illusion that you are doing something great and far more important.

We are not saying here that occasionally following a strong inner urge to substitute your morning routine with another activity will topple all you have worked to build. But we are warning you that in being casual about your morning routine, and following your flow instead of your morning routine, you may leave yourself vulnerable to generating resistance with its accompanying avoidance and procrastination. The end result of even one deviation could be no more morning routine and finding yourself back where you started.

The only good that can come from replacing your morning routine with another activity and allowing the temporary 'high' to motivate you to continue to abandon it, is that you will ultimately reach a point where that 'high' dissipates. Only then, when a sense of emptiness and chaos ensues, will you come to appreciate your morning routine and recognize its invaluable contribution to your life. I say that having gone through this process myself, as have a number of my students.

In summary, following your morning routine on a regular basis ensures your continued receipt of its many benefits. However, if you experience a rare, compelling urge to replace your wake-up program with another activity, it could signal a creative breakthrough or important inner guidance. If you do choose to follow the urge, understand the risks and be prepared to apply whatever inner discipline is necessary to get back to your usual wake-up schedule the very next day.

In the final chapter, we will review what we've accomplished thus far and give you a grand send off with a special gift.

# In Conclusion

We have journeyed far, dear night owl. I feel honored by the trust you placed in me and I congratulate you for your courage and motivation in becoming the best you can be. You learned the true meaning and importance of a morning routine and how to respect who you are with your unique attributes. You learned the components of an effective morning routine and how to customize them to suit your needs. Furthermore, in taking the essential steps of designing and installing your personal wake-up ritual, you bravely confronted your resistance and learned how to engage your brain power to help you overcome and persist.

This is no small accomplishment. Undoubtedly, you are reaping the benefits of your morning routine and feeling more powerful in your life. Know that with these tools, nothing is beyond your abilities; every dream is within reach. Be confident that your persistence will pay off in ever-increasing success and well-being.

If you have read this far but are still hesitating, please know that there is nothing to fear. It's not too late, so why not give it a try? Start small by adding just one new step to your morning schedule and build from there. What can you lose when there is so much to gain?

Like you, I'm a night owl who once had a dream of starting my day in the most powerful way. But for a very long time it was only a dream until I finally took action. Now it is my everyday reality, and with the help of the information in this book, it can be yours as well.

Before you go, please make sure to visit https://bit.ly/troubleshootingresistance/ for your free gift, "Troubleshooting Resistance: How to Deal with the Stress of Change and Stay on Course to Achieve Your Goals." This bonus report is a transcript of a presentation I gave to a group of my students. It contains essential information for overcoming the natural human tendency to resist change, and helps make it easy and fun to install and maintain your morning routine practice.

# Did You Enjoy This Book?

Dear Reader,

Thank you for reading *Morning Routine for Night Owls: How To Supercharge Your Day With A Gentle Yet Powerful Morning Routine!* I hope you enjoyed it. My purpose in writing this book is to offer night owls the support, information and techniques that will help them adapt and thrive in a 'morning person' world.

If you would like to recommend this book to other readers, please write a brief review on Amazon now. It will only take a few minutes, and I would appreciate it very much.

Thanks again, and wishing you the very best!

*S. F. Howe*

# Books by S. F. Howe

## MIND · BODY · SPIRIT

HIGHER CONSCIOUSNESS

### Matrix Man
How To Become Enlightened, Happy And Free In An
Illusion World

The author reveals a new reality paradigm that will
liberate you from the limiting beliefs and programs
that prevent a joyful and fulfilling life. Available in
print and digital editions.

### The Top Ten Myths Of Enlightenment
Exposing The Truth About Spiritual Enlightenment
That Will Set You Free!

. Essential reading for spiritual seekers. What no one
else will tell you to help you avoid the many pitfalls
of the spiritual journey. Available in print and digital
editions.

### The Bringer Discourses
On Waking Up To The Mind Control Programs Of
The Matrix Reality

For those seeking freedom from cultural
indoctrination, this book offers a higher dimensional
perspective on the most ingrained and unquestioned

aspects of everyday life, and has the ability to heal and awaken humanity. Available in print and digital editions.

PLANT INTELLIGENCE

### Secrets Of The Plant Whisperer
How To Care For, Connect And Communicate With Your House Plants

A plant whisperer reveals the hidden truth about plants and why relating to them in a conscious way is vital for their health and well-being. Available in print and digital editions.

### Your Plant Speaks!
How To Use Your Houseplant As A Therapist

Let your house plant solve your problems! Discover the little known art of receiving life coaching from your favorite indoor plant.
*Coming Soon!*

PERSONAL GROWTH

### Vision Board Success
How To Get Everything You Want With Vision Boards!

A powerful technique for achieving goals and manifesting your desires. Available in print and digital editions.

## Sex Yoga
The 7 Easy Steps To A Mind-Blowing Kundalini Awakening!

A technique for activating the chakras to induce a powerful kundalini experience. Available in print and digital editions.

## Morning Routine For Night Owls
How To Supercharge Your Day With A Gentle Yet Powerful Morning Routine!

Morning rituals aren't only for morning people, and they don't have to be rough and tumble or performed at top speed to set up a perfect day. Welcome to the world of the gentle yet powerful wake-up routine for night owls! Available in print and digital editions.

CONSCIOUS HEALTH

## Transgender America
Spirit, Identity, And The Emergence Of The Third Gender

A higher consciousness perspective on the transgender agenda; what it is and why it is being rolled out at breakneck speed to social engineer a gender dysphoria epidemic. Available in print and digital editions.

## When Nothing Else Works
How To Cure Your Chronic Lower Back Pain Fast!

The simple method that no doctor will ever tell you about. Requires no drugs, no surgery, and no special equipment. Available in print and digital editions.

# About the Author

S. F. Howe is a transformational psychologist, author and spiritual teacher. Howe began teaching psychology at the university level while a doctoral candidate in clinical psychology, and went on to work in hospitals and clinics for more than 25 years as a psychotherapist, staff psychologist, clinical program consultant and director of chemical dependency and psychiatric programs.

In the midst of graduate studies, a profound spiritual awakening led to a complete reevaluation of the author's life path. Thus began a spiritual journey along the road less traveled, extending far beyond clinical psychology, conventional reality paradigms and both traditional religion and new age spirituality.

While engaged in a unique, ongoing process of discovery, the author enjoys sharing with others an ever-expanding understanding of the true nature of reality. This has resulted in

Howe's noted books and teachings on the subjects of higher consciousness, conscious health, personal growth and plant intelligence.

Howe's primary intention is to bring an end to suffering by guiding others on a well-worn path to truth and expanded awareness.

Many of those who have experienced Howe's input and presence report emotional and physical healing, life-changing realizations and dramatic personal transformation.

S. F. Howe may be contacted for speaking and teaching engagements. Please direct all inquiries to: info@diamondstarpress.com.

# Free Gift

As my thanks to you for reading *Morning Routine for Night Owls: How To Supercharge Your Day With A Gentle Yet Powerful Morning Routine!* I would like to give you the important bonus ebook, "Troubleshooting Resistance: How to Deal with the Stress of Change and Stay on Course to Achieve Your Goals."

Offered exclusively to readers of *Morning Routine for Night Owls*, this free report will enable you to overcome the resistance and procrastination that tends to arise sooner or later when you attempt to make lasting changes in your life. It is essential reading because it will give you the tools to stick with and reap the benefits of your new morning routine.

To download your bonus gift, go here now: https://bit.ly/troubleshootingresistance/